Above: Her unique style, p36. *Right:* A dream childhood, p8

Above: Becoming the Duchess Of York at her Royal wedding, p14. *Left:* The King abdicates, p22

Right: Family at peace, p20

Left: Her daughters step back and Her Majesty the Queen Mother shines, p80

D0925062

HM Queen Elizabeth, The Queen Mother is published by *Express Newspapers*
Ludgate House, 245 Blackfriars Road, London SE1 9UX. Telephone 020 7922 8000,
Printed by Polestar, Watmoughs. Copyright *Express Newspapers* © 2002
Permission to reproduce all pictures and text can be granted only by prior written agreement
Special thanks to Colorific!, Camera Press, Express Syndication, Hulton Deutsch, PA,
Syndication International, and Tim Graham

Those little children who, just last August, waited outside Clarence House to present their birthday posies to a friendly old lady in a pretty dress and hat could not begin to guess at the memories behind the sweet smile that greeted them. Few of us could – despite the fact that we regarded the Queen Mother almost as a member of our own family. We had learned to take her for granted: an eternally sunny, fun-loving, gracious, interesting and interested personality. Now she is gone. And it is only now we see just what a remarkable woman she was. One of the most remarkable, perhaps, in a remarkable century.

The often-quoted fact that Queen Elizabeth the Queen Mother was as old as the century itself has resulted in telling contrasts of public and private life. Her idyllic Edwardian nursery years could have been scripted by the writer of *Peter Pan*, JM Barrie. The First World War that claimed her brother was declared on her 14th birthday. As the General Strike brought twentieth-century Britain as near as it ever came to revolution, Elizabeth was recovering from the birth of its future monarch. She spent her 40th birthday fretting, like every other wife and mother, about her family's safety in time of total war. And, when she reached pensionable age, she and the century entered their lively sixties together – both equally dedicated to the cause of the younger generation.

And now, the woman who joined the world at the end of the 19th Century leaves it in the early part of the 21st.

Contemplating the eventful life of Elizabeth Bowes-Lyon as we look forward to a new age, the words of William Shakespeare come to mind: 'We that are young shall never see so much, nor live so long.' An epitaph for a tragic king is strangely apt for a Queen whose whole life, though touched by tragedy, was dedicated to joy and bringing joy to others.

There is no question that Elizabeth Bowes-Lyon would have been a unique blessing to any family. Intelligent, lively and fun-loving, tigerishly devoted to her loved ones and courageous in a crisis, she would have been a wife, mother, grandmother and great-grandmother to be proud of, to adore. As it happened, the family she married into was in particular need of her special gifts.

Bertie, George V's second son, was a stammering nonentity in whom few saw potential for great things. Those who did, however, agreed everything would depend on his future partner. 'I do hope he will find a nice wife who will make him happy,' said Elizabeth's mother after Elizabeth first turned him down. 'I like him so much and he is a man who will be made or marred by his wife.'

When Bertie fell for Elizabeth's bright, sweet nature, he may not

Unfading charm: little Elizabeth Bowes-Lyon, known to locals at Glamis as The Princess, grew up to be a Queen and Britain's most loved Royal

have realised the great strength of character that lay behind it. His great good fortune was that this strength was to be placed wholly at his service. She helped him face his responsibilities as Duke Of York and, in perhaps their greatest crisis, his unexpected role of King. More than this, she provided the happy home that was so important for his development into a confident and considerable statesman. The Royal Family faced the threat of Nazi invasion not as head of an imperial dynasty but as a family,

as determined as every family in Britain to stand together and face whatever Hitler threw at them.

With the war over and the King's untimely death, her Royal duties might have dwindled. In many ways, however, they had just begun. She had a major role in training her family to be Royal – grateful for the privileges and brave about the burdens. And more than anything she taught by example. 'Work is the rent you pay for life,' was what she preached – and practised.

So anyone who attacked the monarchy had to first take on the Queen Mother. It seems hardly possible that a woman should dedicate her life to public service while giving every indication that the whole thing had been tremendous fun.

In a lifetime that's had its bad times as well as its finest hours, Her Majesty the Queen Mother never gave anything less than her best, anything less than total commitment to her beloved nation.

An appointment with destiny

When Queen Victoria died in 1901, no one could have guessed that in the Hertfordshire nursery of Lord and Lady Strathmore was a baby, not yet six months old, who was to prove as significant for the destiny of the Royal Family in the twentieth-century as Victoria had been in the previous one

As she was not born a princess (she was, however, a descendant of both Robert The Bruce and Brian Boru, High King Of Erin), little Elizabeth Bowes-Lyon could not be expected to figure in the future of the monarchy. But times were changing. The passing of Queen Victoria marked a real break with the past, and the remarkable destiny awaiting Elizabeth Bowes-Lyon reflected this.

But for the time being, Elizabeth enjoyed an archetypal, storybook Edwardian childhood.

Warm, secure, full of love and fun, it produced a sparkling, confident, kindly little girl – a Wendy to heal the hearts of Lost Boys everywhere. The legend that, at a party, she passed cherries from her cake to a tongue-tied little chap sitting next to her – the tongue-tied little chap she would one day marry – is typical of the aura surrounding her. Lord David Cecil, who was besotted for two childhood summers, fell in love at first sight: 'My small damp hand clutched at hers and I never left her side... I had seen and she had conquered.'

Adolescence was not so idyllic. Carefree childhood was cut short in 1914 and Elizabeth's war work was looking after wounded soldiers in her Scottish home at Glamis – not as a nurse, like her older sister, but by running errands and chatting with patients. It can't have been the light-hearted task it sounds. It would not always have been easy to sparkle for the shattered boys and young men who asked for her company – there must have been sights a young girl would rather not see, but duty called. But this early training in what might be called charming for King and country would stand Elizabeth, King and country in good stead in the years ahead.

The conflict over, a sadly depleted generation of young men set about making love, not war – and dainty Lady Elizabeth Bowes-Lyon caught many an eye. Shy Bertie Windsor, awkward younger brother of the dashing Prince Of Wales, was captivated. After the gaiety of the Bowes-Lyon household, his own family life seemed stuffy and dull by comparison. 'No one has the exciting feeling that if they shine, they will be asked again... They know they will be, automatically, as long as they're alive,' he grumbled.

But who exactly had encouraged the sickly, stammering Duke Of York to believe he could, with effort, shine? He had, it seems, been accidentally illuminated by Lady Elizabeth's sunny personality. She may have been taken aback by the ardour of his response – she was certainly not seeking a royal husband. An approach was made and declined. Even the approval of the formidable Queen Mary did not move her. Bertie was in despair.

Then Lady Elizabeth decided – and no one who knew her strength of character doubts it was her decision – that, if asked again, she would, indeed, say yes to his proposal.

'I had seen and she had conquered'

LORD DAVID CECIL

As a young girl, Lady Elizabeth Bowes-Lyon captivated hearts. Lord David Cecil, who was besotted for two childhood summers, was just one fellow that fell in love with her at first sight

Throughout her childhood, little Elizabeth Bowes-Lyon was surrounded by people who loved her and those she loved – none more so than her baby brother David (above and far right). They were especially close because of the seven-year age gap between Elizabeth and their older brothers and sisters (including Mary, pictured holding Elizabeth on the garden wall, top right)

Elizabeth and David were privileged children and lively ones – whether puffing Woodbines in their secret den at the Strathmores' Hertfordshire home of St Paul's Walden Bury; revelling in pantomimes on visits to their London home in St James's Square; or defying ghosts and legendary monsters in the family's Scottish castle of Glamis

Elizabeth always stuck to a gentle, old-fashioned style – a world away from the brittle glamour of the 'flapper' so popular in the 1920s. Instead she had a style of her own – one that the public always adored

Lady Elizabeth was part of the generation of young ladies who 'came out' in the aftermath of the Great War. As the daughter of the Earl of Strathmore (pictured above), she moved in the best circles and won many aristocratic admirers. They found her totally charming, kindly and full of fun – a talented dancer, pianist, singer of popular songs and organiser of high-spirited parlour games

Until Elizabeth Bowes-Lyon, only foreign princesses were considered suitable brides for sons of the King Of England. But when Bertie told his father he wanted to marry her, George V responded by saying: 'You will be a lucky fellow if she accepts you.' She did, and they married on April 26, 1923 (below)

13

Bertie was the first prince to marry in Westminster Abbey since Richard II. The ceremony wasn't broadcast – the Church feared men might listen to it in public houses 'with their hats on'

15

Marriage, motherhood and the monarchy

When Elizabeth agreed to marry Bertie, who was then the Duke Of York, a popular diarist of the day wrote: 'There is not a man in England today that doesn't envy him. The clubs are in gloom.' King George V and Queen Mary were delighted – the 'smiling Duchess' brought a welcome warmth into the bleak formality of Royal family life

O nly the bride's father seemed to have misgivings about the match. He thought Bertie's elder brother, David, was unstable – he might not become King or he might not stay the course. 'Then where would we be?' asked the Earl Of Strathmore. But, in the meantime, the young couple settled down to a happy family life and a light and pleasant rota of Royal duties – on a hugely successful tour of Australia and New Zealand well-wishers offered them three tons of toys for their first baby.

Her daughters were born, not in Royal, but in Bowes-Lyon beds. Elizabeth at 17 Bruton Street in London's West End and Margaret Rose at Scotland's Glamis Castle.

Both little girls – the serious and rather anxious Lilibet and the madcap Margaret – were educated at home and the Duke and Duchess were often spotted wandering down Bond Street or taking a stroll in Green Park from their town house at 145 Piccadilly.

But the family idyll was shattered when, on the death of George V, it became clear the new King, Edward VIII, would indeed not stay the course. Throughout the abdication crisis, Bertie was deeply unhappy at the prospect of becoming King.

Shy and with a pronounced stammer, he was not the public's darling that his brother had been. There was talk in some circles of passing him over in favour of a younger brother to spare both Bertie and his young daughter the burden of the Crown. In the event, though, it was he and his wife Elizabeth who shouldered this unlooked for and unwelcome duty together. 'We must take what is coming to us and then make the best of it,' said the young Duchess Of York.

In a short time, the new King and Queen were called on to show just what they were made of, becoming a family at war. For all of their privileges – Eleanor Roosevelt recalled them eating meagre rations from gold plates – they shared their people's perils. For Elizabeth, the fears of any mother were made worse by the knowledge that her daughters were prime Nazi targets. Sheltering several exiled kings and queens in Buckingham Palace, the Queen zealously practised her pistol-shooting, vowing 'not to go down like the others'.

'So well brought-up, a great addition to the family'

GEORGE V

The perfect love match: The Countess Of Strathmore's wedding present to her son-in-law was a miniature of his Elizabeth (above left). He kept it in his desk drawer till the day he died

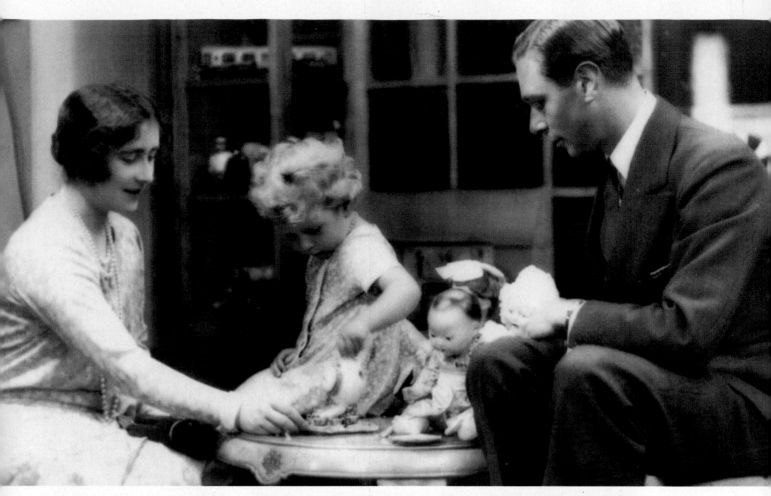

For the Duke Of York, whose own unhappy childhood had left him shy and with a painful stammer, these precious years at 145 Piccadilly were his first opportunity to indulge in the fun of family life

The Yorks' much-loved first daughter Elizabeth (pictured) was not born to be Queen. With Uncle David, Prince Of Wales, still young enough to produce heirs, there was no reason why little Lilibet could not look forward to a well-connected but carefree life. However, her grandfather, George V, was in despair at his eldest son's behaviour. 'After I am dead, the boy will ruin himself in 12 months,' he said

19

The image of the Royal Family as the archetypal, ideal family has taken a battering in recent years. But, in many ways, it was never meant to be a Royal concept – the monarchy has always been plagued by father-son difficulties in particular. But it was a true reflection of the family life Elizabeth created for Bertie and their daughters – a re-creation of the warm and loving family bonds she had forged during her childhood, particularly with her mother and brother David (below)

On December 10 1936 – less than a year after he came to the throne – Edward VIII resigned amid public furore. In his broadcast to the nation, he pledged his support to his brother Bertie, who would henceforth be known as George VI: 'He has one matchless blessing, enjoyed by so many of you and not bestowed on me – a happy home with his wife and children'

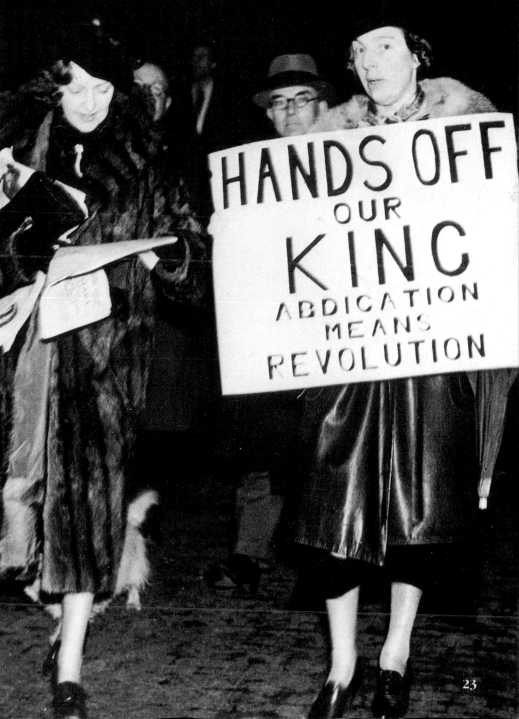

Royal trips, like the one to the visit the Roosevelts in the White House (above), were not idle jaunts but part of a serious quest to win friends and influence people – with the Queen's gaiety, charm and sensitivity vital weapons in Britain's armoury. In France, she placed a single poppy on a memorial to Australia's First World War dead. Watching a newsreel of the event, Adolf Hitler called her 'the most dangerous woman in Europe'

'The children won't leave without me, I won't leave without the King, and the King will never leave.' With these words, Queen Elizabeth dismissed any notion that their daughters might flee to Canada to be safe from the Nazis. They were, however, evacuated to Windsor (right). The Queen almost welcomed the bombing of Buckingham Palace (top): 'It makes me feel I can look the East End in the face'

The Queen took an interest in all aspects of the war effort, giving recognition to unsung heroes. 'The destruction is so awful, and the people are so wonderful. They deserve a better world,' she wrote. The King did his bit too, working two nights a week in a munitions factory. At 18, Princess Elizabeth joined the ATS and qualified to drive and maintain military vehicles. 'We had "sparking plugs" all last night at dinner,' said her proud mother

27

The Queen travelled the country to comfort survivors and thank rescue services after air raids. She robustly defended her decision to look her best even in tragic circumstances. 'They would wear their best dresses if they were coming to see me,' she said, and the public seemed to respond to the courtesy

George VI replied to the message of thanks from both Houses of Parliament when peace was declared: 'I have done my best to discharge my royal duty as the sovereign of free people, and in this task I have been unceasingly helped by the Queen, whose deep and active sympathy for all my subjects in pain or peril and whose intense resolve for victory has comforted my heart never more than in our darkest hours'

After VE Day, the King and Queen toured the London boroughs of Greenwich, Streatham, Lewisham and Deptford, which had suffered so badly during the bombing, and were met by huge, cheering crowds. Like their subjects, the King and Queen held Victory parties, for groups whose war work demanded special recognition

31

Around the time of their silver wedding anniversary (top left), wherever the King and Queen went, they were accompanied by their glamorous daughters – during a visit to the London Palladium (left) or on a trip to Africa (above)

On January 31 1952, George VI and Queen Elizabeth went to the airport to see off Princess Elizabeth, who was heading off for a tour of Africa with her husband, Prince Philip. The King insisted on watching the plane until it disappeared into the distance. Father and daughter were never to meet again...

On February 6 1952, King George VI died. Princess Elizabeth was in the Treetops Hotel in Kenya when she heard the news that she was now Queen Elizabeth II. She flew home straight away to be with her mother, grandmother and sister – all of whom were now her subjects as well as her family. A new Elizabethan era had begun...

A unique style that charmed us

No one could say that the Queen Mother was led by fashion – in fact, fashion simply didn't come into it with Her Majesty. What she had was a personal style, born of her understanding of the function of apparel in Royal image-making. From fairy queen to elegant grandmother, she chose the clothes to suit the role – and the public adored her look

The Queen Mother was always, even in girlhood, passionately interested in clothes and idiosyncratic, not to say eccentric, in her choices. As a young woman of the Jazz Age, she was noticeably and picturesquely old-fashioned in her dress. In the '30s, the glamorous Mrs Wallis Simpson – who thought one could 'never be too rich or too thin', must have looked askance at the Duchess Of York's matronly figure in daywear. But then Mrs Simpson never made it to Buckingham Palace – and Elizabeth did.

It's easy to forget that it was not her daughter's coronation in 1953 but the accession in 1937 of Queen Elizabeth, consort of King George VI, that heralded the New Elizabethan style of royal fashion. The new silhouette was a glamorous echo of the first Elizabethan court, with the full skirts and sparkling jewellery of gowns designed by Sir Norman Hartnell. These she referred to as 'my props'. If the abdication left anyone in doubt about whether the shy man with the stammer was really a King, the sparkling vision dressed in gossamer and diamonds beside him acted as a resounding reassurance.

This functional approach to glamour was most clearly seen in a pre-war trip to France to cement relations. Not since the appearance of Henry VIII on the Field of the Cloth Of Gold had the question of what to wear to impress the French been so seriously considered.

On a 1938 trip to the United States, the Queen won over an influential isolationist politician when she made a special visit, in all her jewels and finery, to his young daughter, who was ill.

As she approached middle age, the Queen Mother achieved a new style for daywear that was both feminine and mature – and then stuck with it. Not unfashionable, certainly not fashionable, it was simply right – a style both instantly recognisable and inimitable.

Elizabeth sparkled in gossamer and diamonds

If there was doubt as to whether the shy man with the stammer was really a King, the vision beside him acted as reassurance

The Queen Mother always gave 'good value' to the crowds who waited to see her throughout her life. Even if it was not the full furs and tiara, there would always be some detail worthy of note

Sir Norman Hartnell's daring designs for the Royal visit to France in 1938 (right) were a triumph. As the Queen was then in mourning for her mother, he chose all-white as an acceptable alternative to all-black. It was said that never had she looked so chic – and her country needed her to do so

As an avid sportswoman – and a Scot – the Queen Mother was never daunted by a drop of rain, and met, with panache, anything the weather could throw at her. When meeting the public, she always made a special effort to brighten a dull day. And when the sun came out again, so did that world-famous smile

41

Well, what is there to say about that famous hat? Quite a lot actually. Like all her choices, this particular style was not only sweet and charming but a shrewd option as well. Designed to give waiting crowds a clear view of her face, it was flattering and friendly. Even if you were too far away from the Royal party to distinguish one Duchess from another, everyone could easily spot the Queen Mother

The Queen Mother was rarely seen in uniform, although she adopted the full pomp for the 1953 coronation of her daughter, Elizabeth II (right).

The Queen Mother, followed by her grandson Prince Charles, clearly enjoyed wearing the flattering and romantic robes of the Garter Knights (left)

On later Royal occasions – such as the marriages of Prince Charles and Prince Andrew – the Queen Mother adopted a more low-key but eye-catching style

To outsiders, this photo could look incongruous: A military ceremony presided over by a smiling old lady dressed as if she were going to open a garden fete. But, like every other British woman of her generation, the Queen Mother knew what war was like, complete with falling bombs and the threat of invasion

The influential family woman

Given the momentous events in her life, it's ironic that most people will remember Elizabeth as she was after the historic cataclysms, such as the Second World War, had passed. Not that her last role – that of Queen Mother – was not in itself historic. Indeed, it proved a vital element of the Royal Family's future development

Widowhood requires an enormous adjustment in any woman's life. For a woman who has been Queen, that effect is almost unimaginable. In the immediate aftermath of her husband's death, Elizabeth's first instinct was to withdraw totally from public life and, as if to give that intention substance, she purchased the remote and ruined Scottish Castle Of Mey as a retirement home and refuge.

It was Winston Churchill who convinced her she still had a vital public role to play. But it was surely affection that drew her back into the family circle. George VI and Queen Elizabeth had followed in a Royal tradition by becoming doting grandparents. For previous generations, happy grandparenthood had been a welcome recompense for the difficulties of parenthood: Lilibet was able to wrap the gruff sailor King George V round her little finger, even though he had been stern and unyielding with his own sons; those sons had themselves, as boys, turned for warmth to grandparents Edward VII and Alexandra, who relished the company of tiny children far more in later life than they had when their own children had been young.

Where George VI and Elizabeth broke with tradition was in enjoying the company of their own children as well as of their grandchildren. And when she chose her new title of Queen Elizabeth, the Queen Mother, she was not only avoiding a public image as the Old Queen, she was reflecting a fundamental truth about the vital role she was to play in the development of the monarchy.

As she was not born a Royal, she was, perhaps, especially protective of those members of her family who were destined to rule. Though universally fond of all of her family, she knew that her husband, her eldest daughter and the eldest grandson had extra burdens to bear, and she stood ready to support them as a loyal subject as well as a loving wife, mother and grandmother.

The public had ample chances to witness the special affection between the Queen Mother and her eldest grandchild, Prince Charles, who wrote of her: 'Ever since I can remember, my grandmother has been the most wonderful example of fun, laughter, warmth, infinite security and, above all else, exquisite taste in so many things.'

And there were occasional glimpses of her fascinating relationship with the Queen. On a family trip to the races, captured in the royal documentary *Elizabeth R*, the Queen made a small complaint which drew from her mother the royal equivalent of, 'That's your own silly fault'.

The Queen's plaintive 'Oh Mummy' could have been said by any child to any mother. It was a poignant reminder that, for all its pomp, for all its significance to the nation, the Royal Family really is a family.

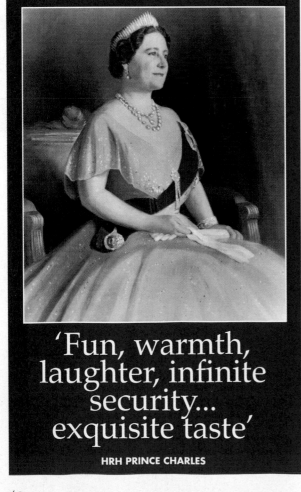

'Fun, warmth, laughter, infinite security... exquisite taste'

HRH PRINCE CHARLES

As she was not born a Royal, she was, perhaps, especially protective of those members of her family who were destined to rule, including a young Prince Charles

Prince Charles's christening in 1948 (below right) was a foretaste of the joy Elizabeth was to find in her first grandchild. 'He was a very kind heart,' she said, 'which is , I think, the essence of everything.' The Prince of Wales had fun in the play cottage (right), given by the Welsh people to the little Princesses Lilibet and Margaret

Charles and Anne were the delight of George VI's declining years (left). When he died, Queen Elizabeth, the Queen Mother – as she asked to be known – realised her grandchildren were going to need her love, support and guidance more than ever

The late Princess Margaret married in 1960 and provided the Queen Mother with two much-loved grandchildren. David (right), who was born in Clarence House, and Sarah (above and right). In the same year as her sister's wedding, the Queen gave birth to a second son, Andrew (above and far right in the Queen Mother's arms)

The '60s were an anxious time for grannies whose grandchildren were reaching their teenage years. Prince Charles, however, seems to have been an exemplary grandson, gradually taking on the responsibilities of his future role (left)

Edward (with cousins David and Sarah, far right) was the Queen Mother's final grandchild and the '70s were, perhaps, her happiest decade – sharing the joys that every granny knows: the new young friends; the carefully home-made gifts (above); and even a dashing new squire (right)

The Queen Mother could take pride in her daughters and her six grown-up grandchildren (below and right). Of the six grandchildren, David and Sarah (pictured above, with the Queen Mother and Prince Charles) had, perhaps, the easiest time growing up out of the glare of publicity

The Queen Mother continued to grace public and private celebrations well into her nineties. With the arrival of so many great-grandchildren, even an intimate family gathering could approach epic proportions – and each year another strapping lad shot up to be able to talk to the Queen Mother face-to-face

59

This sporting life...

It is one of the delightful ironies about the Queen Mother that some of her most famous Royal hobbies and interests placed her four-square with the man in the street. For she shared his love of Britain's most popular sport, fishing, and had, of course, a perfect passion for horse racing. However, they weren't the only games she was happy to partake in...

Horse racing was a favourite sporting outing for the Queen Mother (right and far right) and there is probably no one from whom a winning rider would rather have received a trophy

The Queen Mother had a wide range of highbrow interests, but it's her sporting enthusiasms that endeared her to so many people.

Her career as a racehorse owner was followed avidly by two-bob betters in the bookies – and the disaster when the Queen Mother's horse Devon Lock collapsed just yards from winning the 1956 Grand National showed her best side. With no hint of her personal disappointment, she said: 'I must go down and comfort those poor people.'

And the Queen Mother was not just concerned for the horse's trainer, Peter Cazelet, and jockey Dick Francis. She also made a point of comforting the stableboys – many of whom were, like the jockey, in tears.

But she was not simply attracted by spectator sports. She was keen to have a go herself. Appropriately for a woman who is half-Scottish, she was a keen angler, catching wild salmon well into her retirement years.

It was a strange image in many ways: a woman who has received all the adulation and privileges that it is possible for the world to give; who has met the world's leaders and sparkled in some of the world's most famous jewels – standing thigh-deep in a freezing cold Scottish river in an attempt to catch her own dinner.

Fishing has always been famous for introducing a sense of proportion, a calm amid the hurly-burly of daily life. Perhaps for this reason she made a point of passing on her love of the sport to Prince Charles.

The Queen Mother often surprised with her willingness to be 'one of the lads'. The hand-eye co-ordination of the expert angler could be used at the golf course, the coconut shy or the pool table

The Queen Mother always got delightfully caught up in the excitement of racing – especially when her own horses were running. And the whole family learned to share her enthusiasm

Although she didn't bet on the horses, the Queen Mother had the 'Blower' installed in Clarence House, broadcasting the odds and the runners for the day just as it was heard in betting shops across the land

Homes and gardens

Throughout her life, the Queen Mother sought to create a home-loving and welcoming atmosphere for family, friends and visitors, with cosy interiors and delightful gardens in both town and country. From her early homes, St Paul's Walden Bury and the stunning Glamis, to Clarence House and a humble fishing cottage, she certainly had many glorious abodes

Prince Charles once described his beloved grandmother's knack of 'making any house she lives in a unique haven of coziness and character'

From the very beginning, Elizabeth Bowes-Lyon was a privileged child, with several homes of different styles, each with their own attractions and excitements.

St Paul's Walden Bury meant the soft southern idylls of Hertfordshire; the London house in St James's Square promised metropolitan excitement and trips to the theatre; dour Glamis spoke of drama and romance, with half a dozen ghosts, a legendary monster and a history stretching back to the days of Macbeth.

As a Royal Duchess and then Queen, there had been a variety of homes, some with problems of their own – Buckingham Palace is a cavernous place to get cosy in.

In each house that different circumstances brought her, Elizabeth set to and made as warm and comfortable a nest as possible. Beloved grandson Prince Charles described her knack of 'making any house she lives in a unique haven of coziness and character'.

As Queen Mother, Elizabeth sought a reflection of her childhood homes. For St James's Square, read Clarence House; for St Paul's Walden Bury, The White Lodge and Birkhall; for Glamis, the Castle of Mey.

Happy memories of Glamis (right), prompted the Queen Mother to buy the Castle of Mey – a favourite retreat for younger family members too

Southern belle: As well as her London home at Clarence House (above), the Queen Mother kept on her old family home – complete with its stunning gardens – at the Royal Lodge, Windsor (top right)

Northern lights: The ruined Castle of Mey (right) was bought and renovated soon after the Queen Mother was widowed. Less grand but as loved, the Deeside fishing cabin (left), was an 80th birthday present from her family

Birkhall (top), set in acres of fabulous greenery on the Balmoral Estate, was said to be a favourite of the Queen Mother's for its close proximity to the fishing waters of the River Dee (above)

BIRKHALL

Birkhall is a Scottish dower house that the Queen Mother turned into a welcoming and informal home, used mostly in the autumn. Her beloved brother David was staying here when he died in 1961

The Queen Mother is thought to have chosen Birkhall for its likeness to one of her childhood homes, St Paul's Walden Bury. However, she was also a big fan of all things Scottish and is said to have liked nothing better than whiling away the hours with her family at the magnificent country estate

In town or country, the Queen Mother never lived anywhere without a beautiful garden. It may have been a while since she put hand to spade but there are ways and means. Even the Queen has been spotted weeding on hands and knees when 'Mummy couldn't find a gardener'

The Royal who was 'one of us'

From the time she first won the nation's hearts as the 'smiling duchess', Elizabeth was always the public's welcome guest and one of the world's favourite Royals. In a unique way, she combined the aura of someone who was really special with that of a friend, an interested visitor to whom you could confide anything

Once, at a regimental ball, a young officer was dancing with the Queen Mother when she spotted a friend and stopped to say hello. As she was chatting, the Queen arrived and the hapless young man was dragged away by his commanding officer and told to ask Her Majesty to dance. Having finished her conversation, the Queen Mother turned to look for her partner and saw him dancing with the Queen. 'Snob,' she called after him, laughing, as he spun past with his new partner.

The Queen Mother was not a snob. She could be, when occasion demanded it, but that's not the same thing at all. From an early age she had been trained by her mother, the former Nina Cavendish-Bentinck, in the real meaning of the term 'social graces'. 'Life is for living and working at,' she was told. 'If you find anything or anybody a bore, the fault is in yourself.' And she did not find people a bore. 'That was a real swell queen,' said one GI during the war. 'Talked to me like she was Mom. She was sure interested in every darn thing, even my old man's stomach ulcer.' This wasn't an illusion. Accounts by ladies-in-waiting and palace officials testify to the difficulty of keeping her to a tight schedule of perfunctory handshakes with no chat.

Any movie star may have the knack of making you think that meeting them is the most exciting thing that's ever happened in your life. The Queen Mother could make people feel that meeting them was one of the more exciting moments in hers. During the war, on a visit to a nursing home, Queen Elizabeth was told that, when she heard about the visit, an old lady had touched up her carpet, scrubbing with red ink and a toothbrush. As she shut the door behind her, the Queen was overheard to say: 'What a lovely red carpet.' Calculated? Perhaps. But calculated for someone else's benefit, not for her own. As Osbert Sitwell said: 'She would always instinctively and with grace find the right thing to do at any moment.'

She could strike up a rapport with old and young alike. One November's day she came across a seven-year-old girl who had fallen off her bike in Windsor Great Park. She climbed out of her Range Rover and, with a tissue, gently mopped blood and tears from the child's face.

Another time, the Queen Mother was being mobbed by a party of Italian tourists near her Scottish home, the Castle Of Mey. Displaying a little-known facility for languages, she surprised them with an affectionate 'Buon giorno!' to accompany her usual cheery and, by now, customary wave.

Aristocrat, queen, empress, she took more pride in simply being a good woman. In the words of an East-Ender who saw her hold a baby for a mother who had been injured in an air raid: 'Oh, ain't she lovely; ain't she just bloody lovely.'

'That was a real swell queen'

AN AMERICAN GI

The watchword of any meeting with the Queen Mother was respect. Not the respect that other people felt for her, though that was great, but the respect with which she treated them

World War II was known by many as the People's War. Elizabeth, taking a keen interest in everyone involved in the conflict, was the People's Queen

Ironically, the Queen Mother often paid visits to old folk who were younger than she. As well as a gracious visitor, she was a useful reminder of the potential of older people

The Queen Mother, who lost a brother in World War I and had helped so many soldiers back to health at Glamis Castle, could share many memories with the old soldiers at Chelsea Hospital (right)

Young at heart

'She had a young spirit, great courage and unending sympathy whenever and wherever it was needed – and such a heavenly sense of humour.' These were words the Queen Mother wrote about her own mother, Lady Strathmore – and generations of children can testify that both the gifts and the young spirit were passed on to her daughter Elizabeth

The natural respect the Queen Mother displayed for others was not restricted to adults – and children noticed. 'Oh, what a polite lady,' was one little boy's first reaction. It is sometimes possible to find a very young child with a very old soul. By contrast, the Queen Mother's soul never seemed to lose its youthful sense of fun as the years went by.

She revelled, it seems, not only in the childhood of her own children, their children and their children's children, but in that of other people's children too.

As time went on and her public appearances became increasingly rare, the birthday tribute, an opportunity to receive home-made posies from tiny hands, remained a particular source of joy to her.

'Oh, what a polite lady'

AN ENGLISH SCHOOLBOY

As Duchess of York and later Queen, the Queen Mother always had a cheerful word to charm a child. She also had a friendly wave and smile that somehow seemed to be aimed directly at you

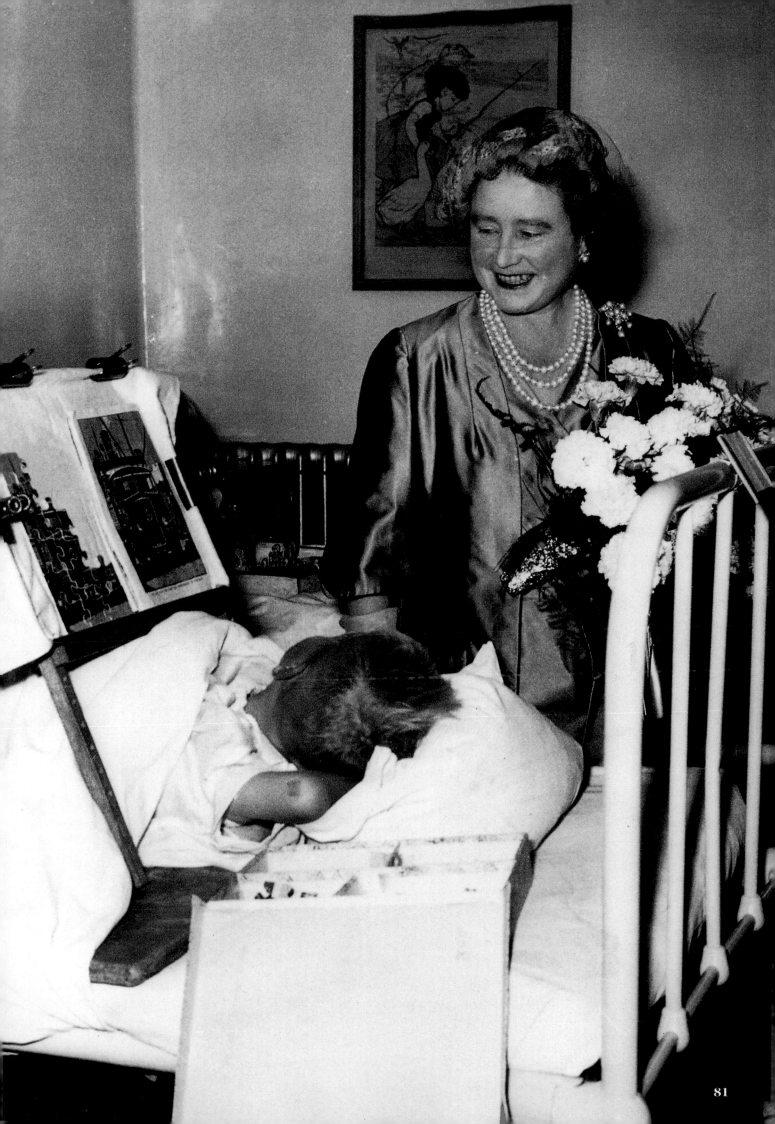

A friendly wave and smile that somehow seemed directed at you is a memory that a remarkably high percentage of Britain's population continue to cherish

The end of the Empire –but still a role to fill

The immense changes wrought in the past century were never more visible than when the Queen Mother travelled abroad. As Duchess of York, she had visited the outposts of Empire; as Queen, she had seen the Empire start to become the Commonwealth; as Queen Mother, she helped to seal the bonds of affection between a family of nations

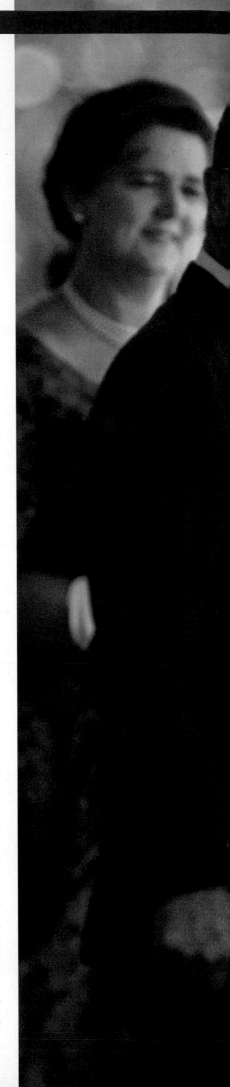

When Peter Pan says 'To die would be an awfully big adventure,' J M Barrie adds: 'Or so he thinks. If he knew more about it he might say "To live would be an awfully big adventure.'" Little Elizabeth Bowes-Lyon, who so loved JM Barrie's plays, did know more about it, did say that – and it was a big adventure

Born a Victorian, into an Empire on which the sun never set, Elizabeth could have inherited the prejudices of her time, her class and her nation. But her ready human sympathy ensured she accepted difference as a source of delight rather than a cause of division.

More than once on their 1947 tour of South Africa, for example, she made a point of defying their hosts' attempts to keep black well-wishers away. One incident marred that visit: a Zulu bystander rushed up to the Royal car and thrust his hand at Princess Elizabeth. He was giving her a birthday gift but the Queen, fearing an attack, defended her daughter stoutly with her parasol, breaking it. Some might laugh it off as an understandable mistake and,

indeed, a courageous response, but the Queen Mother was mortified. It says a great deal about her attitude that she later referred to the incident as 'the worst mistake of my life'.

As a former Empress as well as Queen, her official visits to far-flung colonies played a vital role in helping to smooth the transition from Empire to the Commonwealth that was to become one of the most passionate commitments of the present Queen.

You can see, too, that her attitudes have helped form her grandson's commitment to a multi-racial, multi-faith Britain. 'I have never known her miss church on Sunday, even in the depths of Africa,' said a friend. 'She has been to some pretty erratic services, but it's all God to her.'

In her fifties, the Queen Mother launched into a vigorous programme of world travel, including visits to Uganda (left) and Kenya (right). She took a spin in the first passenger jet just days after its inaugural flight (below)

The Commonwealth, like the Empire, stretches across the globe and it was down to earth transport in Australia (left)

Even in her eighties, the Queen mother was an enthusiastic traveller, in the Channel Islands (above), enjoying an 80th birthday trip in Concorde (left), in Caen, France (below) and in Berlin (right)

OUR AMBASSADOR

From the palaces of Britain to the Palace of the Doge, the Queen Mother went everywhere... and where better for a grand lady than the Grand Canal in Venice

Our favourite birthday girl

Crowds would line the streets, children would come bearing gifts and everyone would know that it was that time of year again. August 4, the day when one of the nation's best-loved Royals celebrated her birthday. Every year, no matter how frail, the beloved Queen Mother would enjoy her day with a massive grin, taking time to chat to waiting fans

The gifts of flowers and special paintings from youngsters livened up every August 4 for the Queen Mother and, too, for her many young fans

It was the Royal event of the century that many loyal subjects also saw as one of the most exciting of the past 100 years. On August 4, 2000, the Queen Mother celebrated her 100th birthday and was cheered on by a crowd of 40,000 people as she appeared – to rapturous applause – at the front of Buckingham Palace.

In a series of celebrations, all dedicated to the nation's most beloved and adored Royal, the lady once known as Elizabeth Bowes-Lyon was given a birthday that many, for generations to come, will treasure for the rest of their lives.

As the week kicked off with many ardent admirers visiting Clarence House to show their admiration and respect for her, the Queen Mother's childhood home, Glamis Castle, played host to a congregation of 3,000 with a special *Happy Birthday* serenade by one of her favourite singers, the Forces' Sweetheart Dame Vera Lynn.

All attention was soon focused on the breathtaking celebrations though, and, indeed, the birthday girl herself. Starting the day at Clarence House, after the King's Troop Royal Horse Artillery had ridden past, the Band of the Irish Guards marched past – joined by Grenadier Guards, playing *Happy Birthday.*

When she was presented with a 100th Birthday card from the Queen, the Queen Mother asked her personal equerry, Irish Guards Captain William de Rouet, to slice open the envelope with his sword. Chuckling as she read the card sent to all centenarians, she was touched to see it personally signed by her daughter with the signature Lilibet, her childhood name.

And, as the Queen Mother and Prince Charles set off for Buckingham Palace in an Ascot landau decorated in her racing colours, she was escorted along a route that took in Stable Yard Road and Cleveland Row – the entire time being cheered on by the assembled crowds.

Following a 41-gun Royal Salute which the Queen Mother watched with wide-eyed glee, she joined 30 members of the Royal Family for a celebratory lunch in the Bow Room of Buckingham Palace.

The highlight of the day for many Britons though was its culmination. The Coldstream guards struck up to the tune of *Congratulations*, the crowd started cheering and the Queen Mother took to the balcony with her daughters.

On her special day, and surrounded by her family, the event seemed to sum up who the Queen Mother was and what she signified in all of our lives.

The world had been blessed with a very different leader: a tough but gentle lady who was ready to fight to the death for her country, but one who also remembered the words to all the old songs and was not ashamed to show it; a granny with a kind smile for the young; and a veteran who took pleasure in sharing memories with the old.

As her family surrounded her on the balcony, it was time for the Queen Mother to step into the limelight once again. The 'People's Queen' was seen for what she was, the heart of the nation. And a presence that will be very sorely missed.

Pictured (right) on her 100th birthday, the Queen Mother chuckles as she opens a card from her daughter, HM The Queen – a message sent to all British centenarians

As the nation goes into mourning for one of Britain's brightest gems, the Queen Mother will always be remembered as a unique, gracious and very special lady, whose death has left a huge void in all of our hearts